Valleys

I0177159

By Natasha Vizcarra

Library For All Ltd.

Library For All is an Australian not for profit organisation with a mission to make knowledge accessible to all via an innovative digital library solution. Visit us at libraryforall.org

Valleys

This edition published 2022

Published by Library For All Ltd
Email: info@libraryforall.org
URL: libraryforall.org

This work is licensed under the Creative Commons Attribution-NonCommercial-NoDerivatives 4.0 International License. To view a copy of this license, visit http://creativecommons.org/licenses/by-nc-nd/4.0/.

Library For All gratefully acknowledges the contributions of all who made previous editions of this book possible.

This book was made possible by the generous support of Save The Children.

Original illustrations by Public Domain images & Creative Commons Licensed Images

Valleys
Vizcarra, Natasha
ISBN: 978-1-922827-99-9
SKU02705

Valleys

What is a valley?

A valley is low-lying land between two hills or mountains. Rivers and streams often flow through valleys.

Kinds of valleys

Valleys are formed in different ways. Rivers and streams can carve out grooves in a landscape. These grooves can grow wider and deeper.

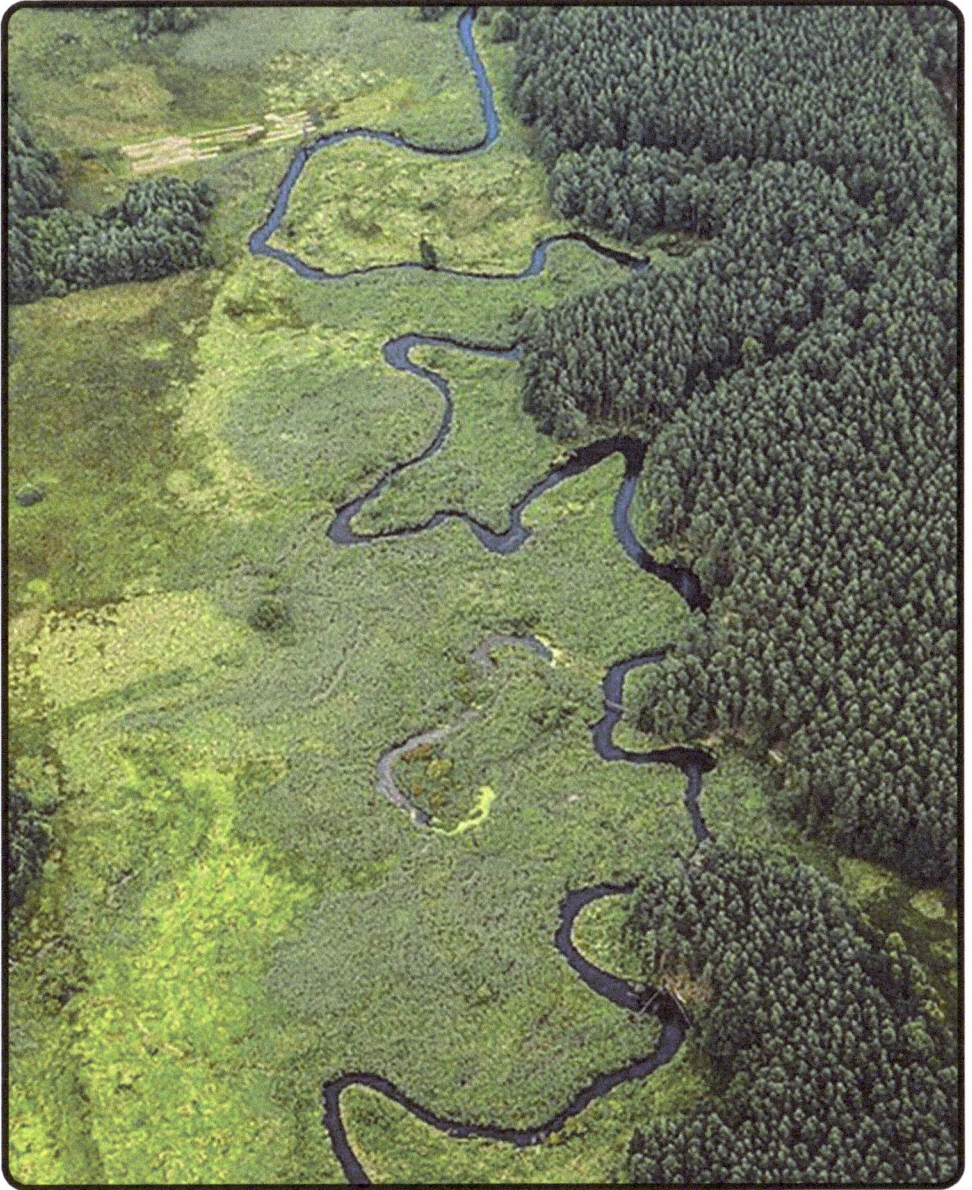

Over time, the grooves become a valley. These are called v-shaped valleys. The curve of the land is shaped like the letter V.

The Black Canyon of the
Gunnison National Park
in the United States is an
example of a v-shaped valley.

Slow-moving rivers of ice, called glaciers, can also carve out valleys. These are called u-shaped valleys because the curve of the land is shaped like the letter U.

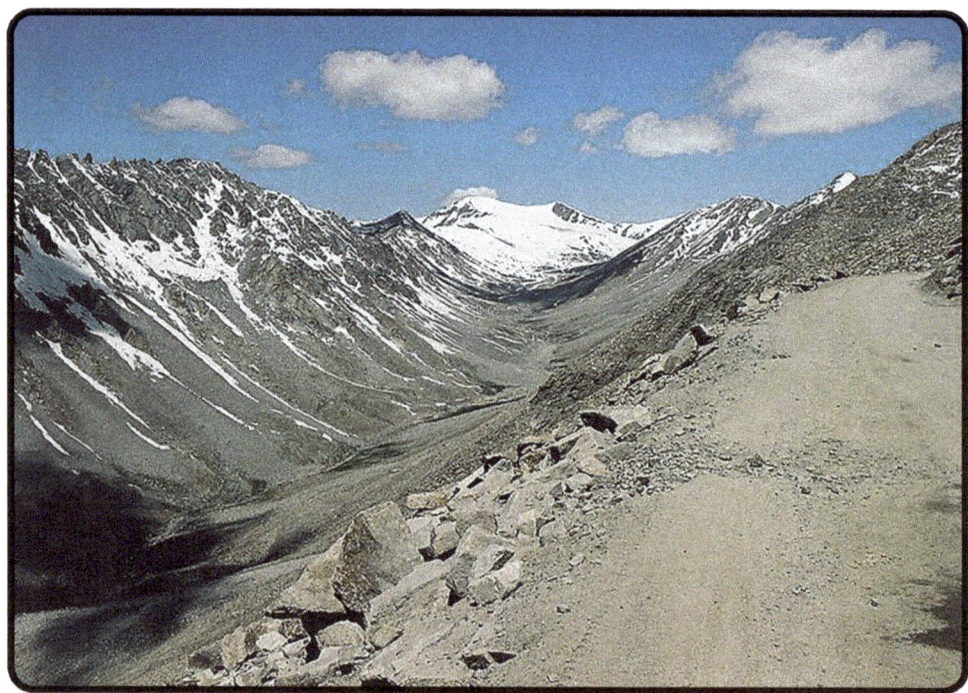

The Leh Valley in India is an example of a u-shaped valley.

Sometimes, valleys are formed when two pieces of the Earth's crust separate or split apart. These are called rift valleys.

The Western Rift Valley in Africa is an example of a rift valley. It is where Lake Tanganyika is found.

People and valleys

Valleys are great places for people to live in. The soil found in valleys is often fertile, making it a good place to plant food.

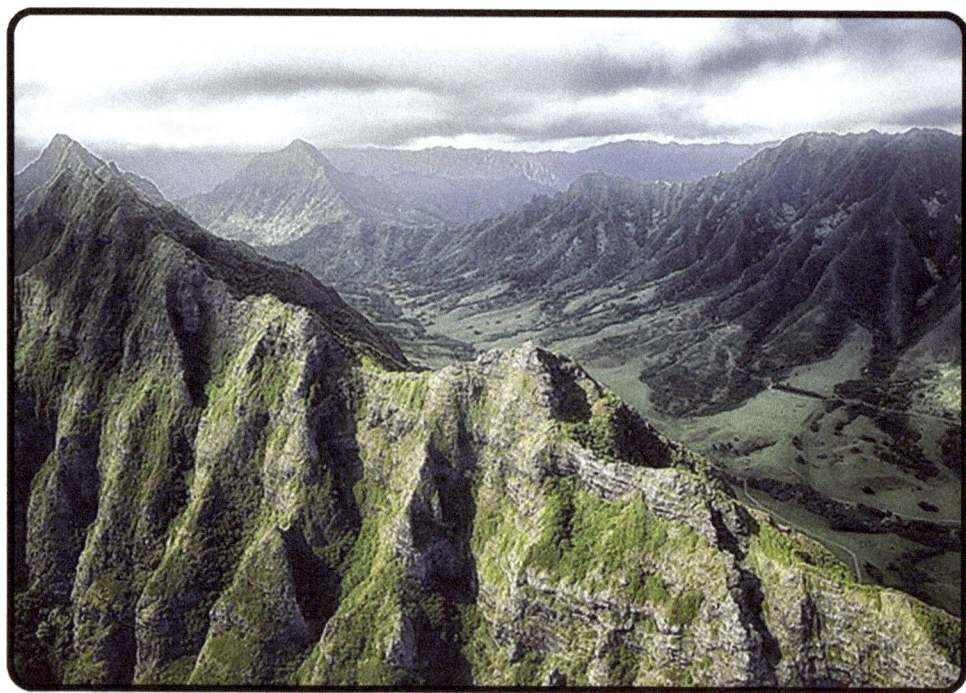

The surrounding mountains or hills also protect the valley from storms.

Valleys around the world

1. Kathmandu Valley, Nepal

2. Indus Valley, Pakistan

3. Valley of the Kings, Egypt

4. Valley of Flowers, India

5. Loire Valley, France

6. Shenandoah Valley, USA

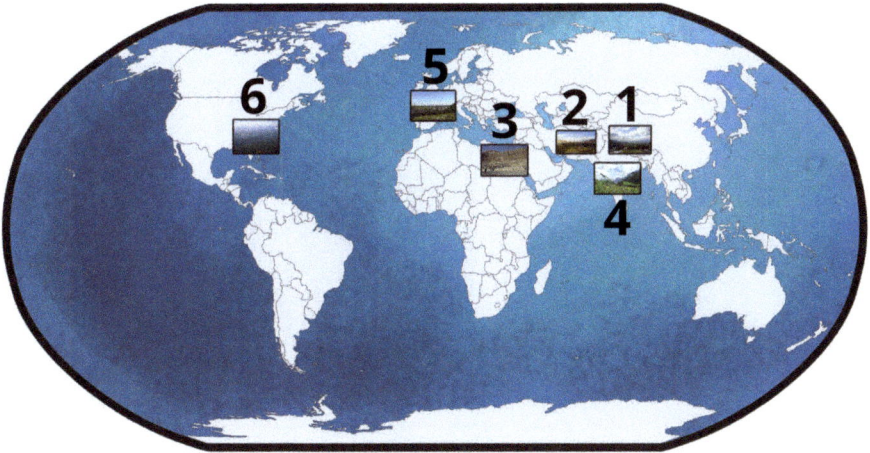

Indus Valley, Pakistan

Loire Valley, France

Valley of the Flowers, India

Valley of the Kings, Egypt

Kathmandu Valley, Nepal

References:

- http://simple.wikipedia.org/wiki/Valley http://mocomi.com/landforms/
- http://en.wikipedia.org/wiki/Black_Canyon_of_the_Gunnison_National_Park
- http://en.wikipedia.org/wiki/U-shaped_valley#mediaviewer/File: U-shaped_valley_at_the_head_of_Leh_valley,_Ladakh.JPG
- http://famous101.com/famous-valleys-in-the-world

Glossary

Fertile: capable of producing lots of plants, fruits or trees

Glacier: a slow-moving large mass of thick ice in extremely cold areas

Groove: a long, deep track on a surface

Rift: a craft, split or break in something

You can use these questions to talk about this book with your family, friends and teachers.

What did you learn from this book?

Describe this book in one word. Funny? Scary? Colourful? Interesting?

How did this book make you feel when you finished reading it?

What was your favourite part of this book?

download our reader app
getlibraryforall.org

About the contributors

Library For All works with authors and illustrators from around the world to develop diverse, relevant, high quality stories for young readers. Visit libraryforall.org for the latest news on writers' workshop events, submission guidelines and other creative opportunities.

Did you enjoy this book?

We have hundreds more expertly curated original stories to choose from.

We work in partnership with authors, educators, cultural advisors, governments and NGOs to bring the joy of reading to children everywhere.

Did you know?

We create global impact in these fields by embracing the United Nations Sustainable Development Goals.

libraryforall.org

www.ingramcontent.com/pod-product-compliance
Lightning Source LLC
Chambersburg PA
CBHW040314050426
42452CB00018B/2838